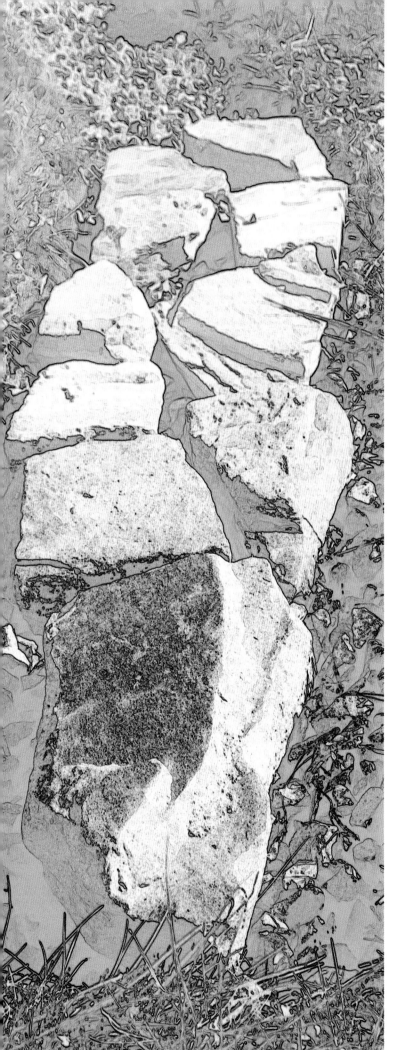

Building Dry-Stack Stone Walls

A. Robert Gallagher
Joe Piazza
Sean Malone

Schiffer Publishing Ltd®

4880 Lower Valley Road, Atglen, Pa 19310

Schiffer Books are available at special discounts for bulk purchases for sales promotions or premiums. Special editions, including personalized covers, corporate imprints, and excerpts can be created in large quantities for special needs. For more information contact the publisher:

Published by Schiffer Publishing Ltd.
4880 Lower Valley Road
Atglen, PA 19310
Phone: (610) 593-1777; Fax: (610) 593-2002
E-mail: Info@schifferbooks.com

For the largest selection of fine reference books on this and related subjects, please visit
our web site at **www.schifferbooks.com**
We are always looking for people to write books on new and related subjects. If you have
an idea for a book please contact us at the above address.

This book may be purchased from the publisher.
Include $5.00 for shipping.
Please try your bookstore first.
You may write for a free catalog.

In Europe, Schiffer books are distributed by
Bushwood Books
6 Marksbury Ave.
Kew Gardens
Surrey TW9 4JF England
Phone: 44 (0) 20 8392-8585; Fax: 44 (0) 20 8392-9876
E-mail: info@bushwoodbooks.co.uk
Website: www.bushwoodbooks.co.uk
Free postage in the U.K., Europe; air mail at cost.

Designed by RoS
Type set in New Baskerville BT

ISBN: 978-0-7643-3056-8
Printed in China

Dedication

This book is dedicated to Rob's wife, Rachel, whose help and support resulted in the successful completion of this project. She has been an inspiration in Rob's life and her positive attitude is contagious.

Thank you!

Acknowledgments

Corporate assistance

Thank you to all of the companies who helped make this book possible. Your assistance allowed it to happen. We can attest to the fact that these companies are full of exceptionally good people who are committed to meeting the needs of their customers each day. If there is any way that these companies can help you in your project we strongly encourage you to give them a chance.

Brandywine Quarry
151 North Church Street
Parkesburg, Pennsylvania 19365
(610) 857 4200

Dupont Company
Wilmington, Delaware

Gap Power
5399 Route 30
Gap, Pennsylvania 17527
(717) 442 8970

Iron Hill Green house and Garden Center
Iron Hill Road
Delmar, Delaware
(302) 846 3122

Pinnacle Stone Products, LLC.
3001 Lower Valley Road
Parkesburg, Pennsylvania 19365
(610) 593 7625

The Odds & Ends Company, Inc.
(610) 368 2377

Personal Support and encouragement

The following people have given us direct and indirect encouragement and support which drove us to complete this book. Thank you for your steadfast faith in us.

John Conner and his family, Bill and Adrianne Gallagher, George Gallagher, Will Gallagher, John Hanaway, Lynn Hanaway, Cameron Malone, Eva Malone, Ann Piazza, Willy Stoltzfus.

The Sweat

Thank you to the following people, who helped us build the three projects that are featured in this book. We appreciate your hard work in making these projects come to life.

Josh Davis, Floyd Lee, Greg, Rachel Gallagher, George Gallagher, Will Gallagher, Kevin Kerr, Keith Kerr, Perry Lyons, Camron Malone, Eva Malone, Robbie Patterson, Wes Penfield, Andy Sperber, Craig Sperber, Kevin Sperber

Photos

The following team of photographers contributed to this book.

Rachel Gallagher, Joe Piazza, Rob Gallagher, Kari Dandrea, Sean Malone, Floyd Lee

Gallery Photos

Thank you to all of the families who allowed us to photograph their fantastic walls as examples to inspire others.

Contents

Fortress on the Ring of Kerry County, Ireland.

The view inside the Staigue Fort, an Iron-Age Dry Stone Fort that is 1,500 years old.

The main passage tomb at Loughcrew or Witches Hill in County Meath, Ireland. Passage tombs in Ireland are estimated to be at least 5,000 years old. Anthropologists believe these tombs were some kind of ancient time piece. For about fifteen minutes a year, the sunlight at dawn comes down the passage and illuminates the central chamber. There are no people buried there, but it is thought that the tombs were part of the ceremony for the spiritual departure of the dead.

The entrance to the tomb. Notice the size of the stone above the doorway to the passage, which leads to the center of the mound. Wonder how they got that stone into place all those years ago...

Introduction

Building stonewalls is a simplistic process, however, it is truly an art to build a wall that is stable enough to pass the test of time. The purpose of this book is to give you the basic procedures needed to build a long-lasting and attractive wall out of dry-fitted stone. In addition, we will give advice to make your projects easier and safer.

The concept of building walls out of stone without the use of mortar has been around for at least 5,000 years. Over the years, they have been used for everything from fortresses and tombs to borders for gardens. There is something very comforting about the basic solidity of stone.

This book is divided into three general sections based on the size of the stones used to build the walls. One-handed stonewalls are made with stones that the average person could pick up with one hand. These walls are ideal for borders for small gardens and along walks, as seen below.

Two-handed walls are built of stones that the average person can handle with two hands. Walls built with this size stone are commonly used worldwide. Stones at this size are used for all of the purposes of one-handed walls plus large dividing walls for yards and pastures, retaining walls, dams, ditch walls, and foundations, as seen below and at the top of page 8.

Finally, we will look at how to build boulder walls, which are made out of stomes that are too heavy for one person to lift. These walls are almost always built using some kind of equipment. These walls are generally used for large retaining walls, large structures like buildings, pyramids, larger dams, larger retaining walls, and drama.

That's right…drama, because there is no way of looking at a boulder wall without uttering, "Wow."

We hope that you either use this book as a guide to build a wall with your own hands or as a way of keeping your contractor honest. In the latter, please note that if you are going to use this book as an evaluation of the work of a local professional, then it is imperative that you realize that there are regional variations in the way that stone walls are constructed.

For example, in areas of Ireland where the sub-strata (under-ground) is made of peat with a thin layer of dirt above, all dry stone walls are built on a concrete base. The concrete base acts like a giant snowshoe so the wall doesn't fall apart as the ground moves beneath.

If someone is building a stone wall in southern Delaware, the base stones can be laid directly on the surface of the ground. The reason for this is that the soil type is sandy and the frost line does not go very deep. The sandy soil type will allow for rapid drainage below the wall, which will reduce or eliminate the chance of ice forming below the wall and heaving the wall out of position. Plus the sand is already compacted, so the addition of the weight of the wall will not make the ground settle.

Only a local professional will know all of the modifications that need to be made to the procedures in this book. They usually learn about the needed variation, because they have failed at previous projects. In those instances, they would figure out the reason for the failure and correct the shortcoming. Be extremely cautious of contractors who wish to use a procedure to build your wall that seems substantially inferior to the procedures in this book. Also try to avoid contractors who have no experience building stonewalls in your area. In most areas of the world, there is no set of common-sense codes that provide a list of how walls should be built based on soil type, stone size, type, use, and climate. The only way to learn about the modification of your procedure is to fail a few times. You need to realize that even a poorly-built wall will look fine for two to three years, before your investment begins to crumble before your eyes.

We hope that you also realize that, if you are going to build this wall yourself, there is a chance—even if you follow every recommendation in this book, there may be a parameter of your project that requires you to alter the procedure to make it work in your area. In preparation, for your project, it would be a very good idea to collect as much local information as you can from code enforcement officers, building inspectors, professionals, and other do-it-yourselfers. Also search your own common sense.

Look, we're not talking about landing the space shuttle; we are making an organized pile of stones. Also keep in mind that making future repairs to dry stonewalls is generally easy, so there is not a large cost of failure. If you follow the procedures laid out in this book, you have an extremely good chance of building a solid wall that will last for decades to come. If anything, you may over-build your wall, making it twice as strong as it needs be.

Chapter One
They're Just Rocks

You are about to learn more about rocks than most people need to know. However, if you are going to be working with rock as a building material, then it is important to know a little bit about rocks. This does not mean that you have to become a geologist to build using stone. Yes, it's going to be a little boring, but we are going to get through this thing together.

There are three main categories of stone on this planet; under each category there are many other named types of rocks. The three main categories are Igneous, Sedimentary, and Metamorphic. When you get down to the local level, a practical way of naming the types of stone is to determine the name based on the town where the quarry is located. In our area, some of the names are, Brandywine Quarry or Parkesburg Stone, Media Stone, and Avondale Stone.

Igneous Rocks

This category of stone is created as molten lava, which has worked its way up into or through the crust of the earth, cools and hardens. What the final type of stone ends up as, depends on what type and combination of minerals is in the lava, along with the conditions of the cooling. The different types of this rock can end up almost any color with a finish that looks like a sponge or smooth as glass. Granite, which generally has a granular look, is one of the most common types of igneous rock.

The igneous rock that cools on the surface is susceptible to weathering, due to its exposure to all that Mother Nature has to throw at it. As the stones are slowly eroded, the wind and rain carry particles away. These tiny particles ultimately end their journey in low-lying areas where run off water can carry them no further.

Sedimentary Rocks

Sedimentary rock starts out as layers of sediment that form in low-lying areas. The sediment may be made up of minerals, crystals, and organic material, like dead plants and animals. Over tens of thousands of years, the low-lying areas get built up with sediment. As time passes, the increasing weight of the layers of sediment above begin to compress the lower layers of sediment together, forcing out moisture and bonding the layers together. Sandstone and shale are two common types of sedimentary stones. You can usually pick sedimentary stones out of the crowd, because the layers of sediment are visible on the cut face of the stone. The first and second projects in this book were built using sedimentary types of stone.

Metamorphic Rock

This category of rock is created when either an Igneous, Sedimentary, or Metamorphic type of stone is subjected to a type of change agent, which alters the appearance and composition of the original rock. These changes may be so great that the initial look of the rock is unrecognizable. Common change agents are heat, pressure, and chemical. Common types of metamorphic rocks are marble, slate, and quartz.

Looking For The Right Rocks

To search out what type of stone you would like to use for your project, there are two main places to get the stones. One place is around your property or the property of a friend. The other is to go to the local quarry or landscape center.

Availability

In either case, there are some things to look for in the rocks that you will use. The top thing is availability. If you don't have enough rock available to complete the project, it may be difficult to get additional stone to match. Usually, availability and cost run hand in hand. Remember that the price of the stone is usually driven by what cost the market will bare and the difficulty in acquiring the stone. Keep in mind that it does cost in time and energy to collect the stones on your own property.

Appearance

Consider what look you want on the face of the wall. Do you want tall rectangular blocks, narrow flat layers, rounded rocks, or some combination of the three? What general color do you want the wall to have?

Workability

If you think that the shapes of stone don't matter, try stacking up 30 bananas versus 30 graham crackers. Which do you think would be easier? Sure, the graham crackers, because they are perfectly flat and have squared edges. The same is true of working with rocks.

The easiest to work with are flat rocks with square break lines.

Irregularly shaped stones are the next hardest to use for building.

The shapes of stone get increasingly harder to work with until you reach virtually round stones, the most difficult shape to use.

Cutting Rocks

In dry-stack stonewalls, the overwhelming majority of the time, you will not have to cut or alter the shape or size of the stones. Usually, you can find a stone or stone combination to fit in a certain location.

However, there are times that the right stone just doesn't seem to exist. So the only thing to do is modify a stone that is close to the right size.

There are several methods to cut your stones to size; score and fracture, chip away, saw cut, and hydraulic cutters. Choosing the right method for the stones that you are using for your project is usually a matter of trial and error. We would approach the trial and error in the order in which the techniques appear below.

Score and Fracture

This is a common method for use on one and two-handed stones of a low thickness. We have used this technique for stones with a thickness of 5 inches. Lets look at the steps.

Using medium intensity blows strike the stone along the anticipated fracture line.

Increase the intensity of the blows and retrace the desired fault line. If the stone doesn't fracture on the second pass, as it did in this case, continue striking with increasing energy along the anticipated break line.

Try the stone for size.

Pearl of Wisdom
We favor the cold chisels that have a plastic safety guard for your hand. Nothing will ruin your day faster than smashing your own hand with a 2-pound hammer.

A cold chisel and a larger hammer can be used for mid-sized stones or for greater control.

The same process can be used for boulders using a wood splitting axe. We recommend that you sharpen the axe before returning it to the neighbor from whom you borrowed it.

Chip Away

The chip-away method is used for adjusting the edge of a stone to bring it to the correct fit. This is a variant of the score and fracture method.

This technique is a little risky; because of the intensity of the blows, there is a chance that the stone could break in an unfavorable way. You still have a better chance of success than you would have gambling in Las Vegas.

Using medium intensity blows, score a target break-line. This merely acts as a guide in this technique, although sometimes you get lucky and the rock breaks right on this line.

Saw Cut

The last method for cutting stones in the field is saw cutting the stones using a gas or electric masonry circular saw. This method is the only way to get it done in the field with larger and thicker stones.

The down side of this technique is that you are left with a very finished cut that may stick out like a sore thumb. The awkwardness of the cut will be determined by the wall design and stone placement.

Mark the cut line on the stone with a pencil, chalk line, hammer strike-line, or scratches. In this case, we are scoring a line with the saw.

Carefully cut along the marked line. Be certain that you use hearing and eye protection while completing this step. There will be an unbelievable amount of both noise and fragments of stone flying around.

Repeated high-intensity blows are used to knock large and small fragments off of the edge of the rock until you reach your target break line. Notice the firmness of the grip on the hammer.

Hydraulic Cuts

If you are lucky enough to live or work near a quarry that is equipped with a hydraulic or other industrial rock cutting machines, then you have another possibility for cutting stones. The only way to know is to ask. Many of these machines have enough power to cut enormous boulders with ease and a high degree of accuracy.

The result.

Always remember that your friends at the quarry are the hands-down experts when it come to handling all aspects of stone. They have equipment and tools that many people have never seen.

The final cut.

Chapter Two
Sticks And Stones Make Break My Bones...

Yes, rocks can hurt you and so can stupidity; luckily there are some simple things that you can do to stay safe. Of course, the number one thing that you can do to ensure that you will not get injured while building your wall is to hire someone else to do it. Even if you have someone else do the work, you should be aware of how to keep people safe on the job.

Safety Gear

There are four items that will help prevent injury when worn.

Gloves

First is a good pair of either leather or leather/synthetic gloves. Gloves are going to help you in several ways. They will keep your hands from being damaged through abrasion. Handling stones all day is similar to resting your fingers on a running belt sander. Without protection, your skin will be eroded away. This feels like a deep paper cut with lemon juice in it. After an injury of this type happens, even wearing gloves hurts for several days.

In addition to abrasion, it will cushion the impact of collisions with rocks in motion. It may not seem like that big of a deal, but even a little cushioning when your fingers are being smashed between two rocks is appreciated.

Finally, gloves will help protect your skin from the elements. Keep in mind that your hands are generally your point of contact with the stones. If your hands are not 100%, then there is a chance of having a secondary injury caused by dropping or mishandling a stone.

Keep your hands in good shape and protect them from injury.

Pearl of Wisdom
This is important because any one of these items will not help you if they are sitting on the tailgate of the truck. You must wear them!

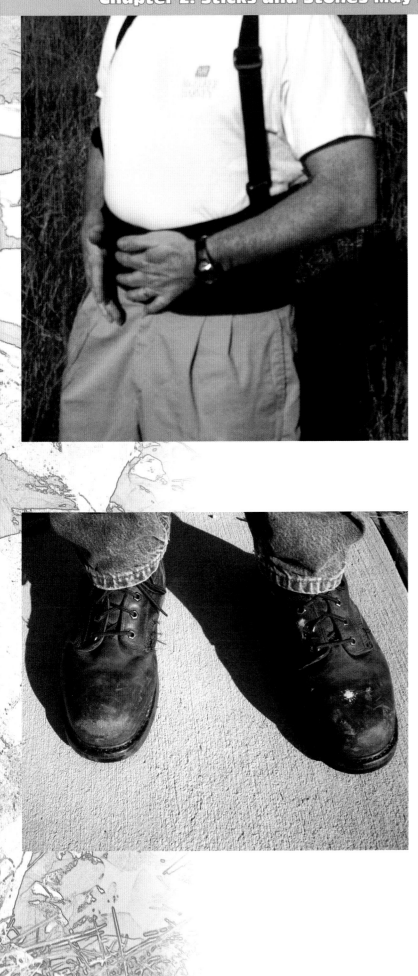

Back Brace

A lumbar back brace is a great way to keep from injuring your back when lifting heavy stones. It will also keep your back muscles from becoming fatigued as quickly. This is because your muscles only have to lift the weight; they don't have to also work to support the bones of the pelvis, low back, and ribs.

There are two things that a back brace will not do for you. One, it will not allow you to lift more weight than you body can physically pick up. In short, it will not make you into Hercules. The other thing that a back brace will not do for you is force you to lift heavy items with proper technique. If you do not lift items with the proper technique, then back brace or not, you are going to eventually injure your back. Please note that proper lifting technique will be covered further on.

Steel Toe Boots

Dropping something heavy on your feet is one of those painful things that give you a life-long memory. We don't know about you, but we have plenty of other life-long memories; new ones of this nature are not needed.

It takes a remarkably small amount of weight to break or smash your toes. We hope you realize that if you are saying, "I wouldn't do something as dumb as dropping a stone on my foot!" then you are almost certainly going to have a stone give you a painful limp. Denial that a safety concern exists merely elevates the chances that it will happen.

The least expensive pair of steel toe shoes that we have ever seen was about fifty dollars. There are also strap-on toe protectors available. We consider this mandatory safety equipment and wear steel toe boots every day to work no matter what kind of job we are working on.

Safety Glasses

Safety glasses are one of those things that people always say you should use, but few people actually put them on. After all, most of the time you really don't need them.

We think that there are three main reasons that people neglect to use safety glasses on a regular basis. First, many times the safety glasses are on the dashboard of the vehicle or in the tool box, and they are not convenient to get your hands on. Second, people tend to buy the cheapest piece of junk safety glasses that they can get. As a result, many times the glasses don't fit well and are uncomfortable to wear. Third, safety glasses get dirty, scratched, and fog up on the job. This makes it nearly impossible to see what you are doing.

My suggestion is that you get good safety glasses that fit your face well and have them hanging around your neck whenever you are working on a project. Also have a clean cloth with you at all times to clean the glasses, as they get dirty. Wear them as much as you can! Even when you feel that you don't really need them.

Safe Behavior

The Dupont Company has a saying, "Safety first, last, and always!" We really believe that safety is a habit. In our company, The Odds & Ends Company, Inc. we have had exactly two hours of lost work for a work-related injury in twelve years. The one person who was injured in all that time ignored my advice about leaving a ladder up against a house on a windy day. Luckily, when it did fall on him, he only ended up with a bruised shoulder and ego.

Safety is all about thinking ahead… What bad things could possibly happen on a particular job site? You must constantly evaluate what things can hurt someone on a job. Listed on page 21, you will see the following things that are potential risks.

Pearl of Wisdom
Of course, the only time that you really need safety glasses is during that one millionth of a second when a rapidly moving projectile pierces your eyeball.

Pearl of Wisdom
Both power and gas can kill you before you get to say "Oh my …"

Four Areas of Risk on the Job Site

Human Risk

Human risks are the potential injuries that are created by a person or people on the job. These occur for the following reasons:

- Individual negligence
- Lack of training
- Lack of common sense
- Taking unnecessary risks to complete a job faster
- Physical or mental fatigue
- The dumb as a post factor

Site Risks

Physical parameters of the job site that create the potential that a person could be injured—things to look for:

- Steep slopes
- Vehicle traffic
- Cluttered work areas
- Buried and overhead services
- Slippery or sharp surfaces
- Other – Every site is different

Material Risks

In this case, the rocks themselves create several different types of risk:

- Crush injuries from falling rocks
- Trip hazards as stones are laid out on the ground
- Abrasion injuries
- Impact injuries from flying fragments of stone

Tool or Equipment Risk

In all of our projects, we used equipment and tools that carry inherent risk:

- Flip hazards with large equipment
- Injuring people who are too close to the equipment in operation
- Property damage caused by operator failure
- Malfunction of equipment causing personal or property damage

Plan For Safety

Do your best to **evaluate the risks** of the job before starting the job.

- Eliminate or minimize the risks that are in your control
- Call the local utilities to mark the underground services
- Take note of any overhead services
- Warn everyone on the job of the location of potential risks
- Make rules for your job to keep everyone safe
- Be diligent about enforcing the rules that you have created
- Keep your job site clean
- Make certain that anyone using tools or equipment knows how to use them correctly

Pearl of Wisdom
There have been many occasions where we have sent someone home, because they were not following the safety rules or they were being reckless. Remember it is your responsibility to keep them safe on your job. The idiot who is taking unreasonable chances on the job site is the same guy who will tell the judge of your negligence in court.

Safety Recommendations for Heavy Equipment

We have many standing safety rules when it comes to heavy equipment; most of these are common sense.

1. If you are unfamiliar with a piece of equipment, practice using it far away from people and structures.

2. No observers within 8 feet of the machine in operation. This does not include persons who are actively working on the project.

3. Stay out of the blind spots of the equipment. If you can't see the operator, the operator can't see you and could kill you.

4. Keep the minimum number of people working near the machine at any given time. Ideally, there will only be one ground person. It is hard for the operator to keep track of the movements of multiple people on the ground.

5. If you are on the ground, keep your eyes on the machine when in use.

6. The operator must be patient; when you rush with equipment something bad will inevitably happen.

7. Safe operators always look where they are going. Never back up blindly, thinking there's nothing there.

8. Never operate heavy equipment when you are mentally fatigued. We like the three-strike method to know when it is time to stop. If you have three mental lapses no matter how small, it is time to take a break. The forth strike is usually painful.

9. Never use broken or neglected equipment, even if it is free. It looses that free price tag when you add in medical costs.

10. Keep a steady lookout for others who may unwittingly stumble into harms way, and warn them.

Remember, a chain is only as strong as its weakest link, so make sure everyone knows how to do his or her job properly. There will be safety risks on your project. Stay on top of things, stay alert, and your project will be a safe and enjoyable experience.

Lifting Safety

It is common knowledge that if you lift heavy objects, you can easily throw your back out, pull a muscle, or even worse, permanently injure yourself. The idea of lifting for some people is to find an object that you need to lift and then hire someone to lift it. Just in case you would like to lift it yourself, there is a proper lifting technique. When done correctly, you can help put substantially less pressure on your back. Learn the proper procedure and do it every time!

To place the stone back on the ground, you would just follow these same steps, but in reverse. You can also drop the stone in a controlled manner; this will help save your energy.

Pearl of Wisdom
Now is the time to make certain that your lumbar brace is on and tight. Even a relatively small stone can fatigue or injure your back.

With all kidding aside, you want to make sure that you are using your legs when you are lifting. Squat down by bending at the knees and keep your back as straight as you can. This is what we call the Duck Squat. Just try that a couple of times. We are having you do this not only to show you the range of motion, but also to help you stretch. Remember that before any lifting, it is always a good idea to do some stretching. Practice on a smaller stone before doing some heavy lifting.

Then, with only your legs, start to gradually and slowly push yourself up, holding the stone close to your body. This is the moment that you will know if you are able to lift the stone. If is too much weight for you, don't be a fool, leave it on the ground.

When your legs are fully extended, rest the stone against your body for leverage.

Chapter Three
Making A Rock Solid Project Plan

Like any other project, the first step is to make a plan to define exactly *what* and *how* you are going to achieve your goal. The more thorough your plan, the smoother your project will go. Virtually every time that a project goes badly someone will utter the words, "We ran into an unexpected problem."

About 90% of the time, taking the time in advance to check all of your bases, to make certain that they are covered, can avert a major or minor disaster. Always remember that no matter how thorough your plan, things will almost always go wrong. A good plan will roll with the punches.

Poor planning on a project generates the following at a minimum:

- Increased chance of injury
- Multiple trips to the supply house, while your work force sits idle
- Needing a tool that you don't have, which stops your progress in its tracks
- Increased chance of hitting underground services like power, gas, water, phone lines
- Increased cost of project due to overages and wasted time
- Increased stress and all of the baggage that goes with it
- Erode or erase enthusiasm for the project leading to depression

Pearl of Wisdom

Starting a project with a weak plan will generate the same result as withdrawing at least 10% of the cost of your project from your bank in singles. Then, burning each dollar one by one until they are all gone. If you like pain, then the thing to do is skip this chapter and start your project tomorrow.

But it really isn't that hard to make a plan, let me show you how.

Ready...Set...Go

After loosing tens of thousands of dollars to poor planning in the business, we came up with a simple, yet effective way of making project plans. It seems silly, but good planning is as easy as ready … set … go. Don't false start.

Ready...

The purpose of the *ready* stage of the process is to complete all of the cerebral work of getting a plan started. During this phase of the planning, you will complete the following items, usually in this order. The photo examples are from the third project in this book.

Sometimes a more formal drawing may be needed.

By this point you most likely have a very clear idea of the layout of the wall. Now you need to decide what size and type stones you are going to use. Eighty percent of the time, people choose the type of stone that is readily available. AKA …cheap!

However, sometimes the local stone of a particular region may not look right or may be hard to use in the construction of a dry-stack wall. For instance, if the local stones happen to be round and smooth, it will be ten times harder to build a dry wall.

To answer the size question you need to consider the following:

What size stone will fit the scale of the site?

Are you building the wall yourself, or are you hiring a contractor to do the work?

If you are doing it yourself, do you have health insurance?

Can you operate small/ heavy equipment like a skid steer or a mini-excavator?

Do you know what these machines do?

How much time do you have to devote to the project?

If you are hiring someone, what is your budget?

Get some bids. (Please note that it will be beneficial to have better drawings of what you want to build to get your bids.)

1. Look at the location of the wall to be built. Consider various possibilities with the site, even if you have a clear idea of what you want done with the project, many times good ideas come from un-expected sources during this phase. The key is to have an open mind.

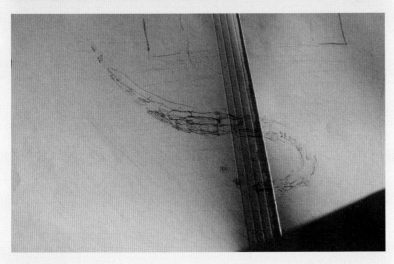

2. Draw a picture of what you are hoping to accomplish. This does not have to be a masterpiece. We have seen many drawings on napkins. Here is the drawing for the bolder project for this book. You will notice that the drawing is on a manila folder. It also is not exactly the greatest picture in the world, if we do say so ourselves.

3. Lay out your idea on the ground with one of the following: rope, garden hose, or caution tape. This allows you to make adjustment to the actual design on the physical location. This is really an important step, because many people can't look at a drawing and envision what the wall is going to look like at the end. Also, this gives you a chance to make subtle adjustments to the design, based on site restrictions and obstructions.

4. Use spray paint or nail your caution tape to the ground, to mark exactly where the wall is going.

SET...

Plan A: Hire a Contractor To Do the Work.

Read this book and others like it. Even though you are not building the wall yourself, this will help in communicating with prospective contractors regarding your job. You will have the terms, the process, and an overview of how the project should unfold. This will help you sniff out a contractor who is planning to learn how to build dry-stack walls by taking a whack at yours. Also, you will be better equipped to spot a contractor who is trying to over charge you by making it sound harder than it really will be to build the wall.

The opposite of that is just as bad, the contractor who is going to charge you what seems to be a fair amount to complete the wall, then takes short cuts on the procedure. You will be able to spot that easily, as the project unfolds. This book will also help you feel quite comfortable with the contractor you choose, as you will be assured that he knows what he is doing.

Hire the contractor of your choosing to complete the job. Ideally, it will be a company that has submitted a fair price for the work to be done and exhibits knowledge and expertise. If you choose people that you like and trust, your project will tend to go a lot smoother. Hire them and let them deal with all of the headaches.

Pearl of Wisdom

No matter what, if your contractor says its daytime out and you have to look out the window to make sure... He is not your guy!

Plan B: You Build The Thing Yourself!

Good for you! It may be a lot of work, but at the end, you will have something that will give you great pride and satisfaction. To get to that touch-down dance at the other end of this project, you have to do some things now. Well, you don't *have* to, but your chances of having a psychotic episode half way through the project increases by 97.64% if you don't.

1. You have to assess your assets and abilities. Get a piece of paper and list how much you want to spend on this project in terms of time and money. If it's a small one-handed wall, this may be a no brainer. On the other hand if your are considering building a 50 foot long, 4 foot high, 2-handed wall with stairs built-in, this may prove to be a valuable step.

When you are considering your time—think about who you could have help complete the project. There are several different places where you can look for help. First is family and friends. You do have to be somewhat careful here, as the help that you are asking from people is hard physical labor. Immediately rule out people who may not be physically up to the challenge, like someone with a heart condition. Another place to find people to help is neighbors or the older children of neighbors. Of course, whoever you get is most likely going to require compensation for their efforts. Another place to look is through your church or other community organizations. Many times, they will know of people who are out of work and would appreciate a way to earn some money. Finally, there are businesses in many areas that sell the use of temporary on-demand labor. This is as close to getting a contractor as you can get, but there is a catch. It is a totally mixed bag of people working for these companies. Some have a good work ethic and some knowledge while others may not be as sharp. Sometimes just having another person working with you makes it like an exercise class. It's better than working out alone!

2. Now you have to weigh how much time you can devote to the project with how much help you can afford to have, based on your budget. The main question that you need to answer for yourself is: Do we have the ability to generate enough energy, personal, and leveraged, to complete this project? If the answer is no, then you need to adjust the scope of your project down to a level that you think you can handle.

3. Determine how much in materials you need to get to complete the job. Think back to school when your Geometry teacher said that this stuff was going to come in handy some day. Well guess what? Today is that day! The good news is that the people who work at the quarry or hardscape supply are more than willing to help you with the calculations. All that you need is to remember the formula to figure out the volume of a rectangle.

Length x Width x Height = Cubic Square Footage.

If you give this number to the associate at the quarry, they can give you a pretty good idea of how much stone to get. Please realize that you need to get about 20% more stone than you think you are going to need. That is because you are going to be assembling a three-dimensional puzzle, and this gives you a better chance of having all of the pieces. The additional stones can be used for other smaller projects or can be given to friends as a holiday gift. On second thought just use them for another project.

For most walls, you are also going to have to figure the volume of the base of the wall. Usually, you will be ordering either ¾" clean stone or modified. Modified type has ¾"-1" stones mixed with "screening" or stone dust. This type of base is better if you are unsure of how solid your soil is at the site. For instance, if you are building your wall in an area that is made up of fill dirt, a stronger base will be more important.

Get a good supply of small flat stone which you will use a "shims" or spacers. This will help you stabilize each stone as you build your wall. Realize that the more shims you have around a stone in a wall, the more stable or "tight" it makes that individual stone and, ultimately, the wall. You want to have a five-gallon bucket full of shim stone of a variety of sizes for each ton of wall stones that you are planning to lay.

4. Look at your job site and make a plan for where materials are going to be piled and how they are going to be handled. For instance, what are you going to do with the soil that is excavated to create the base? Maybe you could have your ¾" base stone dumped right into the dug out footer of your wall. Or maybe the delivery truck can't make it that close to the wall and you have to figure out how to move the stone to where you need it. Make certain that a problem is not being created by putting 20 tons of stone too far away from the job, nor to close. The key here is to have a practical and creative plan. This is an area that can save you a lot of unnecessary toil and stress.

5. Create a schedule complete with a due date or deadline. We find that a good way to create a deadline is to invite friends or family from out of town to stay with you on a certain weekend a reasonable time from when you start the project. Nothing says "get it done" better than judging eyes and a deadline.

6. The final step of the set phase of planning is to create a thorough "to do list" for the projects. For projects large and small, we use a "to do list" that we call a "job matrix," in no small part because it sounds cool. The main purpose of the job matrix is to help you organize the timing of various parts of your project. Many times, we will catch shortcomings in a plan when we apply it to the job matrix. In the absence of something like a job matrix, it is extremely easy to waste valuable time and money in idle thought time during the project. This gets stressful during a job while you are paying three people to look at you while you figure out what to do next.

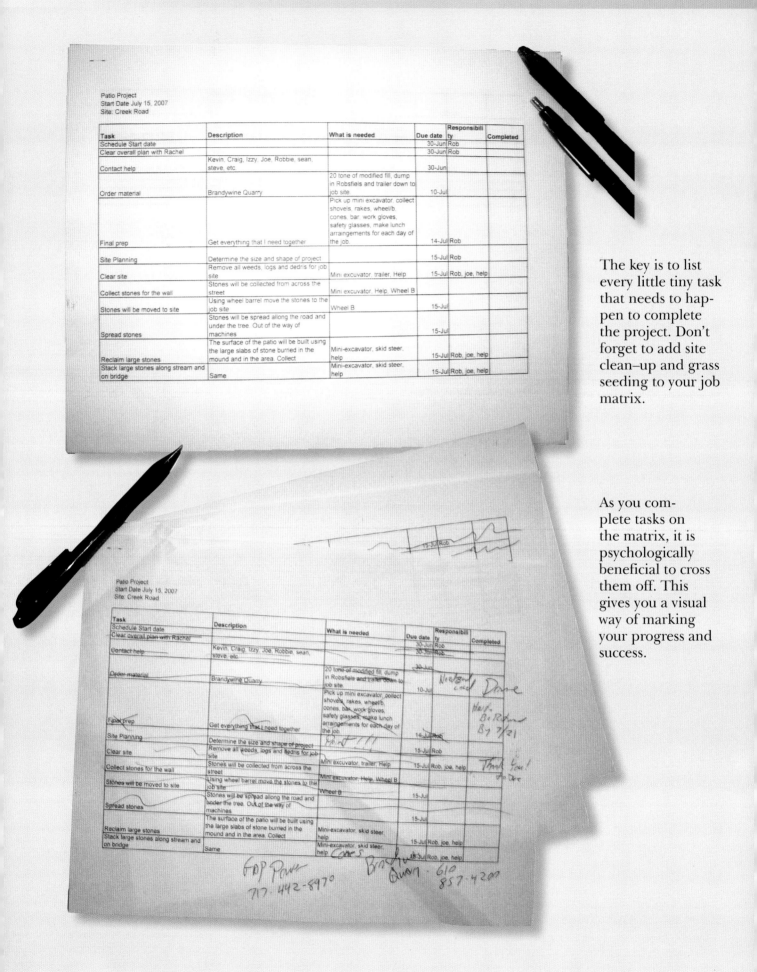

Patio Project
Start Date July 15, 2007
Site: Creek Road

Task	Description	What is needed	Due date	Responsibility	Completed
Schedule Start date			30-Jun	Rob	
Clear overall plan with Rachel			30-Jun	Rob	
Contact help	Kevin, Craig, Izzy, Joe, Robbie, sean, steve, etc.		30-Jun		
Order material	Brandywine Quarry	20 tone of modified fill, dump in Robsfiels and trailer down to job site.	10-Jul		
Final prep	Get everything that I need together	Pick up mini excavator, collect shovels, rakes, wheel/b, cones, bar, work gloves, safety glasses, make lunch arraingements for each day of the job.	14-Jul	Rob	
Site Planning	Determine the size and shape of project		15-Jul	Rob	
Clear site	Remove all weeds, logs and dedris for job site	Mini excavator, trailer, Help	15-Jul	Rob, joe, help	
Collect stones for the wall	Stones will be collected from across the street	Mini excavator, Help, Wheel B	15-Jul		
Stones will be moved to site	Using wheel barrel move the stones to the job site	Wheel B	15-Jul		
Spread stones	Stones will be spread allong the road and under the tree. Out of the way of machines		15-Jul		
Reclaim large stones	The surface of the patio will be built using the large slabs of stone burried in the mound and in the area. Collect	Mini-excavator, skid steer, help	15-Jul	Rob, joe, help	
Stack large stones along stream and on bridge	Same	Mini-excavator, skid steer, help	15-Jul	Rob, joe, help	

The key is to list every little tiny task that needs to happen to complete the project. Don't forget to add site clean–up and grass seeding to your job matrix.

As you complete tasks on the matrix, it is psychologically beneficial to cross them off. This gives you a visual way of marking your progress and success.

Go...

All right now you are ready to *go*. Simply begin to execute your plan as laid out on the job matrix. Of course, there are certain things that you need to do during the project to help it go smoothly.

Focus on keeping a positive attitude about every aspect of your project. It is unbelievably easy for depression and self-doubt to creep into your mind during any project. If you allow this to happen, building your wall will feel like the hardest thing that you have even done. In addition, you will most likely not be a joy to be around. You may even find your help bailing out on you. On the other hand, with a positive attitude even the hardest part of the job will seem effortless.

Always have the ability to **roll with the punches**. In other words, when your plan is crashing and burning, you have to focus on solving the problem—and quickly. Dwelling on what the cause was, whose fault it was, or how unfair it is that the bad thing happened will only increase your pain and suffering.

Keep Your Work Force Happy

> ### Pearl of Wisdom
> *If you have people helping you complete a project, even if you are paying them, we recommend you buy them lunch every day.*

There are two good reasons for footing the lunch bill. Your helpers are working hard for you when they could be somewhere else doing something fun. This shows them that you appreciate their effort. We have even had people who were working slowly in the morning step up their effort in the afternoon. Guilt or self-esteem, we don't care, they worked harder.

The other thing is that it shortens their lunch break. This may not seem like a big deal, but even if people are driving to the Golden Arches they are going to loose one hour of daylight. Let's say you have three people working, that is three man-hours of lost productivity for the day. That adds up psychologically. In addition, when you go to pay your workers, they will most likely take a half hour out of their pay. This is because they are only counting the time that they were off site, not the time it took them to stop and get started again. Many times you can get lunch out of the way in fifteen minutes. You set the time because, when you go back to work, the guilt will force them to do the same.

If you are paying people or buying supplies, do yourself a favor and have the money in hand when it is due. People can justify anything; if you are a slow pay, the main thing you loose is the benefit of the doubt. So if you run short on stone, at say… Saturday at 11:00 a.m., and you have been a prompt pay, there is a chance that the quarry may move heaven and earth to get the stone to you so your project doesn't stop at noon that same day. Do you think you would get the same consideration if you were a slow pay or complained about how expensive the stones were? We don't think so!

Chapter Four
One Handed Stonewall Project

The one-handed stone wall project that follows was built to satisfy a need to create an elevated flower bed with a stone base along one side of a pool enclosure. In addition to making the pool area look better, the flower bed will help keep grass clippings and other debris out of the pool. This project will point out that it doesn't have to be a huge project to look good and make a difference.

The first step is to look at the site and think about what you want the wall to look like. Sometimes, it's hard to see the possibilities.

Extend a water hose
roughly across the site.

Using the
hose, you can
try an infinite
number of
shape options.

We choose to go with the straight-line design.

If you are doing a straight line wall, to insure that it is parallel to something else, in this case the fence, measure the same distance away from the fence, at each end.

Pour chalk along the line of your hose to mark it on the ground.

Hammer stakes at each end of the chalk line.

Tie a line between the two posts, this will insure that you have a straight line for the face of your wall.

Go to the center of the fence. Measure the distance away from the fence to the line, to insure that the measurement is the same.

As you can see, the actual straight line is demonstrated by the string and indicates that the hose was not in a straight line. If this step is skipped, there is no way to know if the wall will be straight.

Using a power-tiller, we loosen the surface of the soil approximately to the depth of the thickness of the stones we are using.

Use the string line as a guide for the tiller.

Then we finish our first pass with the machine.

Now we start the pass with the machine on the rear side of the bed.

At the conclusion of the tilling, we are left with loose soil that needs to be shoveled out.

The soil will be loaded into wheel barrels and used as fill dirt elsewhere on the property.

Take great care in cleaning out the corner of the base.

Usually, when your stones are delivered, they are dumped into a large pile. Using a wheel barrel, move the stones closer to the jobsite.

Make sure that the tire on your wheel barrel has enough air.

Spread the stones out to see what you have, and so you can pick out the right stone.

Now we are ready to start laying our first stones. We usually start by laying the corner stones. Using a wooden mallet, set the stone in place with gentle taps.

We weren't happy with the first stone we set in the corner, so we pulled it out and put in a different one. This one needed to have soil pushed in below one end to bring it up to level.

Now that we are satisfied with the first stone, we set the rest of the sidewalk side of the base of the wall in the same way, using the sidewalk as a guideline. Notice that you want to have the stones touching and the shape of the stones should generally fit together.

We are happy with the first side, so we are ready to build the base for the front and back walls.

Roll out landscape fabric. This will keep weeds from growing through the small stone of the flowerbed that we are creating.

Place stones on the fabric to keep the breeze from blowing it away.

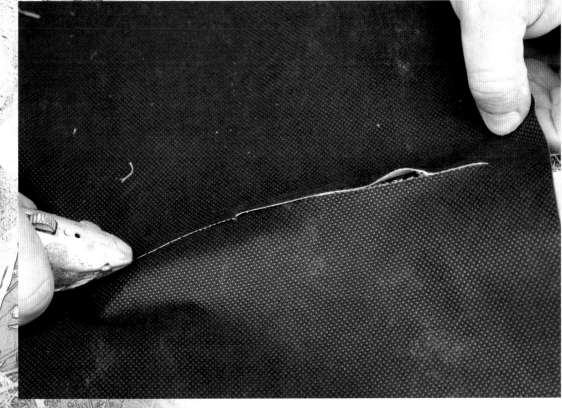

Use a utility knife to cut off the excess fabric.

Now that we have the fabric down, we want to fold it over the base of stones that we have in place. Use the next course of stones to hold the fabric in place.

Continue your second course of stones to hold the fabric in place.

As you continue building your second and third courses, you need to make decisions about each rock, and whether you feel it fits correctly. Here the triangular stone has an uneven height so we decide to replace it.

We replace that single stone with two stones side by side. This picture also shows how the next course of stones went over the replacements.

To level each of your stones, hold the stone level with one hand. With the other hand, slip a small piece of stone (called a shim) under the elevated side of the target rock. This may take a couple tries to get the stone stable. Ideally, for a stone to be stable, you need at least three points of contact.

Build the front wall to butt-up to the fence. At this point the new joins the old and you can see that the old landscape fabric that was below the mulch is still in place.

Here is the completed wall junction at the old wall.

Now that we have the wall built to the height we want, the center is filled with 3/4-inch river rock.

Try to have your fill stone delivered as close to the site as possible. We are lucky to have a dump trailer that we can back right up to our job. This allows us to throw the stone directly where it needs to go.

Now all the stone is in, notice how all our walls and river rocks are covered with dust and dirt.

Start at one end, and with a heavy mist, spray down the walls and river rock. You can see how much stone dust and dirt was on the front wall. Be as thorough as possible with this step.

In the end, this one-handed wall project made a substantial impact on the landscaping surrounding the pool. The project took approximately 30 man-hours and material costs were about $350.

Chapter Five
The Patio Project

The patio project was born out of a need to make a weed-covered knoll into a useful part of the side yard of the home. Initially, we were planning to build a vertical stone wall along the road. Then, when we found the large slabs of stone on and around the knoll, we decided to make the patio. This project will primarily show you how to build a two-handed stone wall with a vertical placement of the stones. This chapter will also show you how to build stairs into a stone wall of any kind.

This patch of weeds is about to undergo a major face lift. It will soon be an elevated patio surrounded by flowerbeds.

The inspiration for the design of this patio project came from this man, John O'Connor, from the Bantry area of Ireland. He was building a "ditch wall" which traditionally is used along roads. He and his crew were working on this fantastic wall when he and Rob had a chance meeting. Before Rob went to Ireland, he'd never seen a dry stonewall built vertically.

The look was striking.

The first step to get to our goal is to use a mini excavator to clear the site quickly.

This mound was covered by a layer of flat rocks that were buried under a thin layer of topsoil. We set these rocks aside to use for the surface of the patio. These boulders are placed in various locations around our job site. Since we are moving these rocks with equipment, some of these stones will be placed from different positions, and scattering them makes this easier.

Even though we called the utility company to come out and mark any underground services on our job site, it is important to note that they do not mark satellite television cables like this. We find this out the hard way on this project.

The next step for us is to mark the outline of the patio with spray paint. We decide on the general shape, but know that the stones would ultimately determine the shape of the patio.

We start by laying down the first stones on the highest part of the existing mound. We spend a lot of time making certain that the stone is level by shimming it with large flat stones.

Then we laid the second stone for the floor. Like the first, we used a skid-steer loader to place the stone in the general position.

With the help of the mini excavator, we maneuver the stone into position. We make certain that the second stone is leveled to the first stone we placed. You will also notice that we have not laid any base stone under the boulders. The reason for this is that the ground was undisturbed, therefore, we were not concerned about settling.

After the third boulder is placed by the loader in the general position, we use the mini excavator to push the boulder up against the ivy covered boulder.

Next, we use the mini excavator's bucket to pull the third boulder closer to the second stone.

After the third boulder is laid, we checked it against the first two stones and found it to be to low.

So, we pull the third stone aside and, using the mini excavator, we bring in modified stone dust to build up the level of the base. Modified stone is a mixture of stone dust or screening and larger stones. This material packs down quickly to form a solid base.

The mound of new modified base is raked relatively flat. Notice that the height of the base is almost to the top of the second stone. This is because we are going to compact the base, as you will see in the next series of pictures.

Using the bucket of the mini excavator, we gently tap the top of the third stone to tamp it down into the new base. We do this repeatedly until the stone is level with the first two.

To lock the first three boulders into place, we fill in around the boulders with modified stone using the mini excavator.

To continue to build the patio, we need to build up the low areas surrounding the original mound. We are doing this with modified stone. Once finished dumping the modified, we used the mini excavator to level the pile.

A garden sprinkler over the new modified stone helps it to settle quickly and minimize future settling of the base.

After lunch, we continue laying the patio in the same manner over the new base. As the stones were pieced together, it becomes clear how each stone will fit into the overall patio.

Many times as we were laying the remainder of the patio surface boulders, we would use the bucket of the mini excavator to lift one side of the stone. Once it was elevated, we threw additional base material under the stone to builds it up to level.

By the next morning, the patio was really starting to take shape. Although we had made paint marks on the ground, the rocks themselves would determine the final shape of the patio.

With the base for the vertical wall ready, we spread out all of the two-handed stones that we are planning to use in the wall.

The next step is to prepare the site for our vertical two-handed stonewall. To do this, we first shovel and rake a small trench around the patio. This serves as the base for the wall.

As you can see, we have a good supply of stone on hand. All of these stones came from the hillside on the other side of the road.

We start the vertical wall at both ends at the same time. The reason for this is that only one person at a time can lay this type of wall, so starting at each end, we can get the wall done twice as fast. We start by taking the bottom course of stones and line them up vertically.

To set the base stones, hold the stones pointed long ways to the ground and tamp it repeatedly until the base seems tight.

Let the stone tip back towards the patio at about 5-10 degrees. At this point, you can see the angle the stones are leaning towards the patio. The one stone that is sticking out is very close to vertical.

Holding the stone in position, pull dirt from the patio and put it behind the stones. This will help hold the stone in place until you can backfill further.

Once the stones are temporarily set with a small amount of back-fill, the next step is to use a shovel to fill the gap between the vertical wall and the patio.

Using a rubber mallet, tamp the fill dirt behind the first course of stones.

To lay a curved portion of the wall, insert small stone shims which act as spacers. The shims should be placed at the bottom front of each of the joints between the stones. This will maintain the wider spacing on the outside of the wall, which will create the curve.

The first course of stone continues around the perimeter of the patio in the same way.

One key in building a vertical wall like this is to use a wide range of stone heights on the first course. In the end, this will make the wall look more interesting because some of the stones will extend to the top of the wall, which will seem to visually "ground" the wall. Plus the various shapes and sizes of the stones increase visual appeal.

Now the puzzle begins. We pick from the stones that have been spread out on the patio. What we are looking for are stones that will fit between the tops of the stone of the first course of the wall. When they are set in place, the top of the second course will be relatively level with the surface of the patio.

Here you can see the shape of the gap between the stones of the wall and the stone in Rob's hand generally fits the shape of the gap.

This stone is in place with many of the other stones of the second course holding it tightly. One great thing about this type of wall is that the sideways friction of the stones being wedged together binds the wall into one unit, even though there is nothing else holding them together.

Notice, at this end of the wall, the ground level comes up towards the level of our patio surface. We gradually reduce the size of the stones on the second course to compensate for this elevation change, until finally, the height of the first course of stones meet the height of the surface of the patio.

It is starting to look like something. Notice that the upper portion of the new wall is being backfilled with modified stone.

In this section of the wall, you will notice that we use smaller stones stacked on top of each other, in some cases three high, instead of having this low area of the wall built with just one course.

The next major component of the project is to build a set of stairs from the patio to the side yard. The top step will be the flat edge of the patio boulder in the lower right hand corner of the photograph.

Using a level and a tape measure, measure the distance down to the ground from a point on the top step of the patio. Once you have this measurement, divide the number of inches by the number of steps that you would like to have. If the number is less than 7.5 inches, then you are set to build your stairs with that number of steps. If you don't know how many steps you want to have, divide the total measurement by 7.5 to see how many steps are needed.

After you have a handle on the number of steps that you are building, the next thing to do is to place your bottom step on the ground facing the direction that you want people to walk. One question that you may have is: How do I know how far away to make the bottom step? The answer is that for each step tread, you need to measure a minimum of 11 inches away from the edge of the top step. In our case, we're putting in four treads. Our bottom step is placed approximately 44 inches away from the face of the top step.

Now that we know where our bottom step is located, it is time to build it up to the measurement of each step, in this case 7.5 inches. We are really building up the front edge of the stone and trying to set the back of our stone into our base material. On this and every tread that you install, check the surface of the step for level; front-to-back and side-to-side. In addition for checking for level, you want to push down on various areas of each tread to insure that you have a tight fit with no movement.

To get the second step started, we place two stones on the back portion of the first step. These stones plus the thickness of our tread stone should be about 7.5 inches.

Note from the shape of our tread stone that the surface of the tread stone is variable. So if you are looking for perfection, you are in for a lot of disappointment. The key is to do the best you can.

You can see from this photograph that we need to lift the back portion of the second tread to make it more level.

To build our third step is a little bit trickier than just putting two stones on the back of the previous tread. In this case, because the second tread is angled and because our third tread is going to turn a little bit, we need to build a solid front support for our third tread.

Here is it from a reverse angle.

Once our third tread is in place, the base supports seem to make a lot more sense. One thing to keep in mind on this, and all other procedures in this book, is that it may take four or five tries to get the stones in a position with which you are happy.

From this overhead shot, you can see how our stairs are slowly turning toward the edge of the patio. The final tread is already in place, as it is the surface of the patio.

Now that we have our stairs built, the next step is to close in the vertical walls around our stairs.

We gradually fill in vertical wall over to the left edge of the third tread. As the wall approaches the steps, we start using smaller stones that match the contour of the tread. We fill in around the backside of the third tread with modified stone, tamping it in as we go.

Finally, the top tread is built into the wall as vertical stones surround it.

The next step is to build a walkway to the patio. The stones are first laid on the surface of the ground.

Next, the soil below the stones is dug out to allow the stepping-stones to be recessed to ground level.

Once the steps are complete, we surround the patio with one-handed border walls to create gardens, and spread mulch over the flower beds and between the rocks on the surface of the patio.

Chapter Six
An S-Shaped Wall—
Part I of the Wall

This wall project was built as a flight of fancy to build interest in an unlandscaped part of Pinnacle Stone Products, LLC, Parkesburg location. Part I of the S-shaped wall project will show you how to build two-handed walls with the stones placed horizontally. In addition, you will learn how to taper the size and elevation of stone to create a taper. You will also learn about laying the base and site preparation.

A panoramic view of the jobsite before work begins.

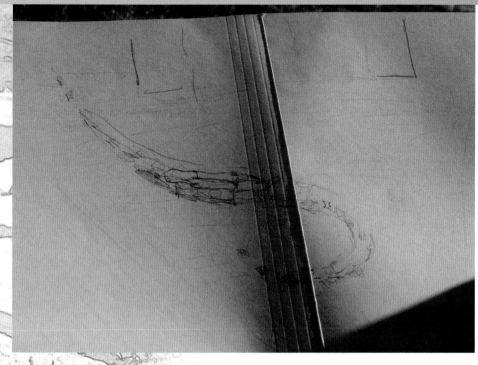

The drawing is used for is to get a general idea of the project across to everyone involved.

Using caution tape, we marked out where the front face of the wall is going to be.

The caution tape isn't staying in place by itself, so we are using 3-inch framing nails, like tacks, to temporarily stick it to the ground.

After being guided into position, he lowers the down-turned bucket into the ground and tips the bucket even further forward to pull the first 8 inches away from the marker tape going 6 inches deep.

The base is dug and the grass is rolled up like carpet next to the trench. Wes did this much with five pulls, in less than seven minutes. This is a great example of how a skilled operator can save you time by fully utilizing the equipment.

After the general work is done with the backhoe, the next step is to go along the tape with flat shovels cleaning up the edge of our trench.

When the edging is done, you are left with a nice clean line which will replace our caution tape markings.

In the portions of the wall that are going to be a one-handed section, the foundation is more narrow and needs to be dug out by hand.

The footer is cleared out by hand, to get it relatively level.

One-handed stones are spread out at each end of the wall. This will help with stone selection as the one-handed portion of the wall is being built.

Finally, the base is raked to insure that we get even coverage with the 3/4-inch base stone that will be laid over it.

Before we start to lay the base, we double-check our measurement to ensure that we have the depth that we need. In this case it is 6 inches.

The base is ready to be filled with 4 inches of 3/4-inch clean stone.

The base of 3/4-inch stone is laid 4 inches deep into the footer trench. There are two main reasons to lay a base like this down. First is to give a solid foundation for our wall, which will not erode and will not be removed by bugs or rodents. Also, it allows surface ground water to drain way from the bottom rocks of our wall. This is important in climates that are susceptible to freezing. Two people can do this process; any more than that, and they will be in each other's way.

Once the guys are finished laying down the stone completely, we move the trailer to the next section of the wall and repeat the process. Notice that the finished fill is relatively flat and even.

It is important for the long-term stability of your wall that the base fill does not come up to ground level. Ideally, the first course of stones should be 80-100% below grade, particularly if the wall is going to be used to retain soil.

Now we are all set to begin laying our wall. We break the total group up into two teams. Work starts at the one-handed taper end of the wall in the front, while the two-handed horizontal wall starts up hill from where the bolder section is going to be in the center of the wall. This strategy is important, because the teams are far enough away from each other that both teams can work efficiently without bumping into each other. Utilizing your work force in efficient work groups or teams is important on a project like this for a couple of reasons. First, if you have too many people working too closely together, they will spend more time bumping into each other than getting the job done. Second, even the best workers in the world will become paid spectators on the job if there isn't enough for them to do. Keep everyone working!

The first stone is laid at the tapered end of the wall. The wall is going to come to a point at this stone.

As you will see in this series of photos, the stones are placed gradually into a spreading pattern, until two consistent lines of stones are evident. These two lines of stone will form the front and rear face of our wall.

For each one- and two-handed base stone that is set, we follow the same process. First you look at the location, the shape and size of the spot where the next stone is going to go.

Then look at the stones that you have spread out on the ground and find one that matches the shape and size that your are looking for to fill the spot.

Once you have made your selection, place it into position to make sure it fits. Notice, the curved contour of the new stone roughly fits the contour of the edge of the existing stones.

The next thing we do to set the stone in place is to *twist* the stone on a center axis while applying downward force. This process compresses the base stone against the bottom of the new rock making a tight fit between the base materials and the rock.

If you feel that the new rock is resting too low, simply tip the rock up with one hand and sweep additional base stone under with the other. Do this a little bit at a time until you are satisfied with the position of the stone.

In the event that the rock you place is too high, there are two things that you can do. First, you can continue to twist the stone on an axis to settle it down into the base stone further. If this doesn't work well enough…

…you can strike the top of the rock with your hand to push it down into the base. You can also use a rubber or wooden mallet to do the same thing.

Continue making adjustments until you are happy with the height of the rock.

We continue laying the front and back base rocks of the one-handed portion of the wall.

Now that the front and back base rocks are set, the next step is to fill in the gap between the front and back base rocks…

…until the first course of rocks is solid from the front side to the back.

Now we can start our second course of one-handed stones.

As you begin to lay your second and every other course, you want to consider the following things.

When thinking about how you want your wall to look, it is sometimes helpful to look at some old examples and ask some relevant questions:

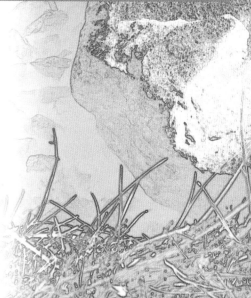

Do I want to have the stones lie in relatively even and flat levels? Do I want to vary the sizes of the stones to add interest? Do I want to throw in a different shaped stone here and there?

We want this section of our wall to look like this when we are done—variable sized one-handed stones with variable joints and gaps.

To get where we want to go on this section of the wall, it is all about stone selection. A lot of time is spent looking through the available rocks to find the one that worked in a specific location.

Here is an example of one location that we are trying to fill. Notice the lower area of the stone on the front side of the wall.

After a few moments of looking, a stone is found that fits just right. The stone is the same shape and the right size. Many times, it doesn't go this easily.

Ideally, stones will be placed so that they cover the joint of the stones on the layer below. The friction between the upper stone and the two stones below will create a bond between all three.

As you continue to lay each stone, make certain that each stone is totally stable. It takes a minimum of three contact points with the stones below the stone you are laying. The more points of contact, the more stable the stone will be. Here, the target stone is stabilized with a shim stone to support the right side of the stone.

After Rob finishes laying the second course of stones, we fill the wall with 3/4-inch stone. Keep in mind that you can also fill the wall with larger stones, modified stone or dirt. This will serve to lock the wall together.

Periodically it is important to lay a stone that bridges from the front face of the wall to the back face of the wall. This stone will help bind the two faces together.

Another thing that helps bind the faces of the wall together is overlapping the stones from the front face of the wall and the back face of the wall. The friction between the two, anchors them together.

Building up the tapered end of the wall. Once completed, this will serve as a guide for the height of the rest of the wall. This is because the wall is going to get gradually higher as you move to the bolder section in the center of the project. This feature of the wall will give the appearance that the ends of the wall are disappearing into the ground.

To begin we lay a stone with a narrowing width over half of the length of the first stone we laid. Then we built the front and rear faces of the wall, so they merge into this stone. From this photo, you can see we have started the third course on the rear face of the wall. The first stone overlaps the narrowing stone at the end of the second course.

This image shows the remainder of the third course as the taper was built with a narrow stone placed next to the first stone for the rear face. We also see the capstone in place for the top of the tapered end of the wall.

Here is how
the completed
taper looks from
above.

The final step in
the tapered end is
to back fill around
the base stone.

Chapter Seven
The Boulder Section—
Part Two Of The Wall

This chapter is the continuation of the S-shaped wall project. Part 2 is the bolder portion of the project. In addition, it is the wrap-up of the entire project. You will learn about handling boulders by hand and equipment. We will also cover the considerations that go into building a boulder wall, including changing your mind.

At this point in our wall project, we are beginning the transition to the boulder section of the wall. This stone at the left is a two-handed stone. The stone at the right is a small boulder, too heavy to pick up, but it can be moved into place.

This photo shows the same stone that Wes had his hand on. The spot in the foreground is where the boulder is going.

To move the stone, it is tipped so the weight is on one point.

The weight of the stone is pivoted on the point until it is footed on the base course of the wall.

When the stone has a solid pivot point on the base rock of the wall, it is tipped towards that pivot point and the (now elevated) end of the rock, is swung into place.

Using the same pivot point, the stone is tipped down into place.

When building a boulder wall, it is critical that each boulder is set exactly the way you want before you move on. Unlike walls made of smaller stones, this wall will be difficult to make adjustments to later. We start by supporting the rear two corners of the boulder. By pushing down on the front side of the boulder, the back is lifted and a shim stone can be placed on the far rear corner.

We shim the near-rear corner to stabilize the backside of the boulder.

Now that we have the boulder stabilized front-to-back, the next step is to level it side-to-side. As you can see, we added a second shim to bring it up to the level that we wanted.

After shimming the rear side, we realize we have created another problem. The stone is no longer level front-to-back. We add a shim to the front-near corner and this solves the problem.

The next technique we use to move big boulders is a long metal bar called a digging bar, used to create leverage. This is a little like a sporting event. The more fired up you are, the easier it will be. We place this boulder as close to the wall as we could with the backhoe, and from here, we use the bar to get it into position.

The first step in flipping the stone over into place is to push the bar as far under the stone as possible and lift it as high as you can. The higher you get it, the better, because the boulder will be closer to its balance point of straight up and down.

You will find that the amount of pressure it takes to hold this stone in place is not that great. We need to hold the stone in position, so we are going to use another rock like a kickstand.

Repositioning the bar farther under the boulder, it is lifted again until stone is straight up and down.

From there is it easy to throw a low block on the boulder and knock it over.

The boulder is in the foundation area, but is not in the correct position. We will demonstrate how to maneuver this boulder using a different stone as an example.

This stone should end up being even with the front edge of the trench. The bar is first pushed down into the bed of stones right next to the edge of the boulder.

The stone can then be moved into desired direction by pushing up and forward on the bar.

The process is repeated one more time to get the stone into position.

Another technique that is important is how to stack one boulder on top of another using a bar and muscle. In this case, we use the backhoe to get the boulder as close as we could. One end of the boulder is laid on top of the base stones of the front-side of the wall. Wes gets the bar under the stone and begins pushing it further onto the base stones.

To get the balance point of the boulder centered over the base stones, the stone is bumped one more time with the bar.

Now that we have the stone balanced in the position that we want, we need to pivot the boulder so that it is set in the right place. One person sets up on the back-side of the stone pushing one direction while another holds it in place from the other direction. Repeated pushes, up and forward on the bar, slowly pivot the stone.

Positions are switched with the back side held while pressure is applied the front.

Once we have the stone within 15 degrees of the position that we want, Wes uses a different technique. He pushes the bar between the stone and the base stone, lifts up on the bar and pushes slightly. The stone will ride on the bar and come to rest a few inches closer to the goal.

Another technique that is important to know is how to use the bar to set up a simple lever. Place a smaller stone next to the boulder and then push the tip of the bar under the boulder. Rest the shaft of the bar on the smaller stone and it will act as a fulcrum. It is extremely important that whoever is operating the bar, focuses *only* on the bar, because if you loose control, it becomes a catapult.

Now that you know all of the techniques for using a bar to maneuver boulders, we hope that you never have to use them. In the next section, we will be using heavy equipment to move the stones around.

The hoe-end of the backhoe is useful moving some of the larger boulders into place. As the old adage says, *use the right tool for the job*. The backhoe had controls that were designed for very heavy digging and moving enormous amounts of weight. These are some of the techniques used to maneuver boulders with heavy equipment.

We place this squared-off boulder onto the first course with the backhoe. Our hope was that the large face of the boulder would act as a focal point for the center of the wall.

To shim the boulder, the backhoe is used to push down on the high point of the boulder and holds it in place with the bucket.

A shim is then placed under the back corner of the boulder. Please note, what earlier would have been a wall stone, is now a shim due to the size of the rocks.

We need to lift the front corner of the boulder to raise it up to level. So we hook a chain on the bucket of the backhoe, run it under the corner of the boulder, and back up.

The backhoe and chain elevate the corner of the boulder into the correct position. Inserted shims keep it there.

The result.

At the end of the afternoon we realized that the backhoe was not the right tool for the job. It was difficult to maneuver in the space; the controls were 'jumpy,' not fine enough. So we decided to rent the correct machine for the job at hand. We made it to the local equipment rental place just in time to pick up the TB-135 mini excavator for the next day. This is a machine we are very familiar with; it has delicate controls, good maneuverability, and plenty of power.

With a mini-excavator, additional stones are laid.

As we continued to build the boulder section of the wall, we used many techniques with the machine to manipulate the boulders to exactly where we wanted them placed.

One technique involves maneuvering a boulder by wrapping a chain around the end of the stone and tugging it into place using the bucket of the mini-excavator.

The first step is wrapping the chain around one of the teeth of the bucket, hooking the chain to itself to create a loop.

The remainder of the chain is strung around the end of the stone opposite the direction it is to move. You will notice that the chain is looped over a small nub of stone, which will help keep the chain from slipping off. The chain is then taken back up to the bucket and around the teeth again, hooking it to the chain to create a second loop.

Tension is gently applied to the chain with the controls of the mini excavator and the stone is pulled to the desired location.

Once the stone has been moved, the chains are removed by simply extending the bucket. The loops fall off the teeth and the chain is free.

A second technique for construction of the boulder part of the wall utilizes the bucket of the machine to push stones into position. You can either position the bucket with teeth pointing toward the ground or extended, and push gently against the side of the stone, using just enough force to move the stone into place.

If you are concerned about marring the stone with the bucket you can retract the bucket and push the stone using the back edge of the bucket.

Let's look at the placement of one boulder as an example of what it took to place most of them.

The first thing that we do in the placement of almost every boulder is to pick it up with the bucket. Begin this maneuver by getting the teeth of the bucket under the far edge of the stone.

Next, retract the bucket while pushing the boom arm straight down at the ground and moving the arm gently towards the machine. It is critical to be extremely gentle and controlled while completing this step because it is easy to damage the machine with one minor lapse in focus.

As you continue to retract the bucket, the stone will find a balance point. Once this happens you can move the stone into any position that you like. It is even possible to lift the stabilizing blade and drive the machine while holding the stone in the air.

With the stone on the bucket it can be aligned with the front of the wall by swinging the boom of the mini excavator at its pivot point, at the front of the machine, and re-aligning the stone to the face of the wall.

Now we are in position to extend the arm out towards the wall, until the stone is hovering over the correct spot.

To release the stone, extend the bucket gently until one edge of the stone is resting on the wall.

In a smooth motion, continue to extend the bucket while lifting the boom. This allows the bucket to rotate at the same elevation, and the stone slides off into the wall.

Reach over the wall with the bucket and gently pull the stone so that it pivots into good alignment with the front face of the wall.

Finally, various parts of the bucket, in different locations on the stone, can be used to push it towards the front face of the wall.

The final view of the stone in place, before any shimming or leveling.

As you can see, the large focal-point boulder on the bottom of the wall, with more narrow stones above, makes the wall seem grounded and not top heavy.

A final look at the wall before the cap course. First, you will notice that the height of the wall tapers up from a one-handed section through the two-handed section, to the height of the boulder wall. Not only is the height of the wall increasing in the areas closer to the boulder section, but also the thickness of the wall is increasing in the same way.

We need to figure out how our cap course is going to tie into the boulder sections at each end. At one end of the boulder section, we have an open gap, as the upper boulder curves away from the lower boulder.

At the other end of the boulder section, the boulder tapers into the level part of the two-handed wall.

Once we have considered the factors that are going to make the cap course look right, then it is time to take measurements of the thickness of the wall in various points. This is very important on this project because the thickness of our wall changes consistently over the entire length by design. It is a good practice to take thickness measurements even if your wall is supposed to be one thickness.

We are quite certain that your memory is perfect, but just in case, write down every measurement that you take, in order.

Now it's time to go shopping and here is the store. Just in case you don't have a pile of rocks that can supply you with 500 times the number of rocks that you are going to need for your wall, it would be a good idea to set some aside for this purpose as your wall is being built.

As we found stones that fit our size requirements, we loaded the smaller ones into the skid steer by hand.

As the sizes of the stones increase, the use of a backhoe to mine and load the capstones becomes necessary.

All of the cap stones are brought close to the wall with the skid steer loader. Then they are spread out on the ground so we could easily pick out the pieces of the puzzle. The larger stones are carried close to the intended position on the wall with the skid steer loader.

It is extremely important to place the capstones on the wall as gently as possible. If you drop the capstone on the wall too hard, it will cause a small shock wave through that area of the wall. The end result is almost always rebuilding the area below the stone.

We tried this stone in two different places on the wall before placing it in this location. It was too wide for the first spot and over hung the wall. It was too narrow in the second spot, but the third place was just right.

Pearl of Wisdom
    It is easy to get in over your head when you are picking up heavy rocks. Keep in mind that the rock has the advantage. If it looses the battle, it gets carried somewhere. If you loose, the booby prize is rating every day for the rest of your life by the degree of pain you are feeling. Have extra help on hand and use it. Don't try to be a hero.

As you may have imagined, the stone didn't float on a cushion of air to get to these other locations. No, we picked it up the old fashion way.

We continue to lay out the heavier stones first. Many of these seemed to have a natural fit in only one location on the wall. This was due in large part to the thickness of the wall.

Once the larger capstones are stabilized using shims, we fill in the remainder of the wall using the smaller capstones. This strategy works well, because the smaller capstones are easier to move and fit in multiple locations.

In a perfect world, every cap stone would fit together in concise even lines. This can be easily achieved using a gas-powered masonry saw that looks like a chainsaw with a circular saw attachment. The look of this wall does not lend itself to perfectly cut capstones.

In our case, we have to make adjustments using the stones that we have available. These two stones are a good example of the two ways that we handle an inherent problem that we have with the natural break of this type of stone.

The left joint of the stone on the left in the prior photo, is handled by placing a large triangular stone as the next cap-stone. This stone serves the purpose of matching one side of the point of the next stone. Plus it bonds the front and rear faces of the wall together.

Once the large stone is stabilized with shims, we lay a smaller triangular stone as a filler stone.

At the opposite end of the same stone we locate a triangular filler stone to fill the gap on the rear side of the wall. This helps to keep the line of the wall a little smoother.

We continue to fill in the remainder of the cap course.

With the cap course complete, there is one more thing that we need to do... fill in the open joints with small shims of stone. This is one of the most important keys to make the wall pass the test of time. It does this by completely eliminating any movement between the stones.

Start by getting a lot of shim stones. For this wall, we will use the equivalent of "two bucket loads" of shims. It is important to have a large variety of sizes and shapes. One key, however, is that the stones need to be wedge shaped. This helps them lock into place as they are inserted.

Begin inserting the shims until you have closed the gap between two stones. Once you have a tight fit, tap the face of the shims gently to set them in place.

Begin inserting the shims until you have closed the gap between two stones. Once you have a tight fit, tap the face of the shims gently to set them in place.

Repeat the process until the joint is totally filled. Keep in mind that the fewer the gaps the stronger the wall.

Now that the wall is complete, there are a couple of things that we still need to do to wrap up the job. The Quarry asked us to run a wire down to the lower part of the wall for future up lighting and an outlet.

If you are running electricity, it is best to do it on the up-hill side of the wall before back filling. The type of wire we ran is 12-2 UF-B, which is designed for direct burial. Here, Wes uncoils the wire being careful not to kink or damage the conductors.

Backfill the uphill side of the wall, which will bury the wire and dispose of the topsoil that was dug up when digging the footer for the wall.

These final photos of the wall were taken upon completion.

The finished wall.

Chapter Eight
Conclusion

In conclusion, your new dry-stack stone wall project should go smoothly now that you have professional, insider knowledge. Operating a safe, efficient project that yields a product to match your vision is a rewarding experience that encourages you to try other projects. Any project that you want to complete has a procedure; all you need to do is follow the procedure to achieve your goal. With the correct tools and some tried and true advice, anyone can do it! Our hope is that you will choose to move forward with your projects and have fun doing it.

This series of books was written to teach you the procedures and the pitfalls in an interesting and light-hearted way. Look for other step-by-step project titles with Schiffer Publishing.

The following photos will give you some ideas that may help you in visualizing your project.

Gallery of Walls

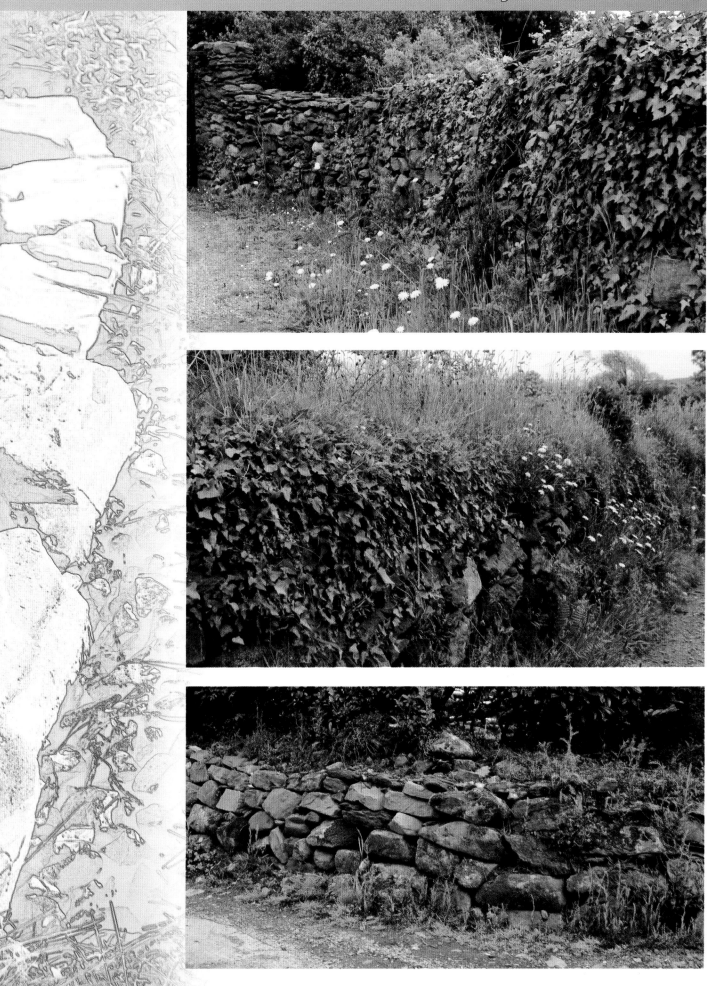